Peter D

Stewart

The Skyscraper Falcon

by Linda Birman

hancock house

ISBN 0-88839-389-X
Copyright © 1997 Linda Birman

Cataloging in Publication Data

Birman, Linda, 1950–
    Stewart, the skyscraper falcon

    ISBN 0-88839-389-X

    1. Peregrine falcon—Washington (state)—Seattle—Juvenile litera-
ture. I. Title.
    QL696.F34B57 1996   j598.9'18   C96-910393-X

Printed in Hong Kong

Editor and Production: Sharon Boglari and Nancy Miller
Front cover photographs: Ruth Taylor
Cover design: Dean Richards

A portion of the proceeds from this book is being donated to The Seattle
Peregrine Project.

Published simultaneously in Canada and the United States by

HANCOCK HOUSE PUBLISHERS LTD.
19313 Zero Avenue, Surrey, BC V4P 1M7
(604) 538-1114   Fax: (604) 538-2262
HANCOCK HOUSE PUBLISHERS
1431 Harrison Avenue, Blaine, WA 98230-5005
(604) 538-1114   Fax: (604) 538-2262
Web Site: http://www.hancockhouse.com   email: sales@hancockhouse.com

Dedication

Foreword

In January of 1995, I took a class on birds of prey taught by Bud Anderson, a local bird expert.

In April, Bud took my husband and me on a field trip to see the wild falcons of Seattle. There I met some of the dedicated members of the Seattle Peregrine Project who volunteer their time to track the progress of the nesting birds.

We had to take an elevator to the top of a tall building called the Washington Mutual Tower. We went into a small room where a TV monitor was set up with a VCR. The monitor was showing a close-up picture of a beautiful peregrine falcon sitting on a nest box. And the picture was live! The volunteers had set up a video camera to peek out of a hole in the wall and look right out at the nest box. The picture was being recorded and broadcast into the lobby of The Washington Mutual Bank located on the first floor of the building. Bank customers could watch the nesting falcons start a new family!

These rare, wild birds had chosen to nest in a spot that allowed us to see the entire nesting process. My hope is that through the work of the Seattle Peregrine Project we can all recognize the importance of this once endangered species living freely among us and that we can appreciate the skill and beauty of this remarkable bird.

Acknowledgments

To the members of the Seattle Peregrine Project and Falcon Research Group who were so generous with their photographs, time and support.

To all the Seattle businesses and organizations who have supported the work of the Seattle Peregrine Project especially Wright Runstad, Washington Mutual Bank and Allied Security.

And finally, to my second grade students past and present who inspired me to write this book and continually challenge me to see the world with the wondering eyes of a child.

To the Reader

This book was written specially for children.

It can be a **read aloud** for young children.
It can be a **read along** for beginning readers.
It can be a **read alone** for more experienced readers.

The first time that scientific words appear they are highlighted in **bold** print. They can be found in the glossary at the end of the book. This glossary will also help you pronounce the word by spelling it like it sounds (phonetically). It will also tell you the meaning of the word.

You will find some questions in this book.
Not all of them are answered.
Think about them. Talk about them with others.

I hope that the story of Stewart and his family will inform and delight you!

This is Stewart. He is a **peregrine falcon**.

Peregrine falcons usually live in open areas on high cliffs, like the one in the picture above.

From their high perches they can see far to hunt for food.

6

Stewart lives in the city of Seattle.

His home is at the top of a high building named the Washington Mutual Tower.

Why would a tall skyscraper in a big city be a good home for a falcon?

Peregrine falcons were one of the first **endangered species**.

In the 1950s people used a poison called DDT to kill insects.

Birds ate those insects, and falcons ate those birds.

The poison made the falcon eggshells so thin that they often broke, as is shown below.

Broken eggs meant no babies.

There were fewer and fewer peregrine falcons.

Then people found the problem and stopped using DDT in the United States.

People worked to help peregrine falcons.

Falcon experts raised baby peregrines in **captivity**, and then when the birds were grown, they were released into the wild.

Some birds were released into wilderness areas.

Some were released in the "skyscraper" cliffs of large cities.

But Stewart was not raised in captivity. He is a wild falcon.

Wild animals don't usually like to live close to people.

That is why his city home is so special.

It lets us see peregrines live wild and free again.

Photo: Patricia J. Hitchens

Photo: C. M. Anderson

Today laws protect peregrine falcons and their numbers are growing.

But DDT is still being used in some parts of the world in insecticides, like the one shown here. Other insect poisons are used in the United States.

Is the danger over for peregrines?

9

Stewart is a **bird of prey**.

A bird of prey eats other animals (**prey**) for its food.

This may seem harsh, but it is nature's way of keeping certain animal **populations** down. This means not having too many of any one kind of animal.

Peregrine falcons are bird hunters. The picture below shows a peregrine falcon carrying a pigeon.

Photos: Martin J. Muller

Stewart's favorite food is pigeons.

Can you guess why?

(Seattle, like many big cities, has a large population of pigeons!)

Peregrine falcons are famous for their exciting hunting style.

They fly high and look downwards for a bird to eat.

When they spot a likely meal, they fold their wings in close to their body and fall in a spectacular dive called a **stoop**.

They grab the bird and nip it in the neck to kill it. After landing they pluck out the feathers and begin to eat.

Photo: Martin J. Muller

Peregrine falcons can reach speeds of over 200 miles per hour in a stoop and are considered to be one of the fastest animals on earth!

They have been called the "cheetah of the skies."

How is a peregrine falcon like a cheetah?

Peregrine falcons, like all birds of prey, are built to hunt.

They have large eyes and keen eyesight for spotting prey.

They have hooked beaks for killing and eating their prey.

Photos: C. M. Anderson

They have four long toes—three in the front and one in the back.

Long toes help them grab their prey.

Each toe ends in a sharp black claw called a **talon**.

Talons help them to hold their prey.

Falcons have narrow, pointed wings for fast flight, as can be seen in this picture of a juvenile peregrine.

Fast flying helps falcons to chase and catch their prey.

13

Peregrine falcons have beautiful markings.

Stewart's head is dark with a wide, black sideburn.

This sideburn is called the **malar** stripe.

He has a creamy white bib, and short black marks on his belly.

The marks going across his belly are called **barring**.

Stewart has a gray back.

Isn't he handsome?

Stewart is called a **tiercel**, which means a male peregrine.

He is about the size of a large crow.

With most falcons, males are smaller than females.

Experts think that the smaller male may be a swifter and more skilled hunter to provide for the family.

This is Bell.

She is Stewart's mate.

She looks like Stewart but she is larger—about the size of a small gull.

Photo: Ruth Taylor

Experts think that the female may be larger in order to better cover her eggs.

This is called **incubating**.

Here is a picture of Bell incubating her three eggs.

Photos: Ray Congdon

This is Stewart and Bell's nest box on a ledge of the fifty-sixth floor of the Washington Mutual Tower.

It is a wooden box filled with dirt and gravel that was placed on the high ledge just for them. A peregrine nest is called an **eyrie**.

Falcons do not build nests out of twigs like other birds. Instead, they make a **scrape** in the dirt and lay their eggs there. The picture below shows a falcon nest scrape.

Photo: Martin J. Muller

In March or April, Bell will lay three or four eggs.

They are about the size of chicken eggs.

They are reddish brown in color.

They will take a little more than a month to hatch.

But not all eggs hatch and not all babies live to be adults.

Both parents will take turns feeding and **brooding** the young.

Brooding means to keep the babies warm.

The baby in this picture was just hatched.

Photo: Patricia J. Hitchens

Photo: Ruth Taylor

Baby falcons are called **eyasses**.

This is related to the nest word, **eyrie**.

The babies have small, white feathers covering their bodies.

These special feathers (called **down**) are very warm, but the babies still need the warmth and protection of their parents.

Eyasses spend a large part of each day resting.

This helps save their energy.

Can you see all three eyasses in this picture?

Stewart and Bell spend many hours each day hunting to feed themselves and their new family.

They tear off small chunks of food, and feed each baby "beak to beak."

The powerful parents, who are fearsome hunters in the sky, are gentle and patient with their babies.

When birds eat, they swallow food into a pouch in their neck called the **crop**. This is a holding place for food.

Can you see the full crop on the first baby in this feeding picture?

A crop is handy for adult birds, too. Adult falcons must often gulp down large amounts of food in a hurry.

They hurry because when they are standing still eating, they are in danger and could become food for other animals. Or their food could be taken away by other animals.

They also eat a lot because it may be a long time before their next meal.

Hunting is not always easy or successful.

Photo: Patricia J. Hitchens

These eyasses were **banded** when they were about twenty-five days old.

A band is a wide, flat, metal ring that is fastened around a bird's leg.

The bands give each wild bird a number and letter "name" so that experts can identify and keep track of individual birds.

Each bird has two bands, one on each leg.

One band is from the United States Bird Banding Laboratory and has a number.

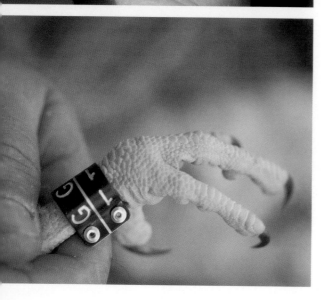

The other band is called a Visual Identification band or **VID band**. This band is black with two white letters, or a letter and a number, that can be seen with binoculars.

People can identify an individual bird more easily when the bird wears a VID band.

Photos: Top: Ray Congdon
Middle: C. M Anderson
Bottom: C. M. Anderson

Photos: Patricia J. Hitchens

These older eyasses look very different from their first baby pictures.

At this age, they can stay on the nest without their parents and are often left alone.

They are growing new feathers. These feathers will help them fly.

They can also feed themselves from the scraps of food left by their parents, but they don't mind being fed by mom or dad.

Peregrine babies make their first flight when they are about six weeks old.

The babies are then called **fledglings**.

The fledglings will learn hunting skills to prepare for the time when they have to live on their own.

Notice how the brown feathers of the young bird on the right are a different color from his parents.

Peregrines do not get their adult gray feathers or **plumage** until they are about one year old.

Young birds in their first year after fledging are called **juveniles**.

Photo opposite: Patricia J. Hitchens

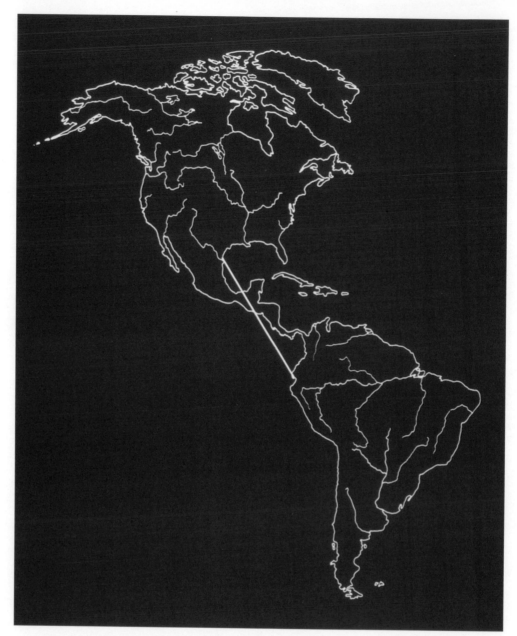

Photo: C. M. Anderson

Some peregrine falcons, like many other birds, **migrate** from one place to another.

Sometimes the birds fly thousands of miles to other lands as shown in this picture.

In the fall, the northern birds migrate south to warmer areas and stay there for the winter.

In the spring, they migrate north back to their nesting sites.

But Stewart and Bell don't migrate.

They stay in Seattle all year. *Why?*

Because they have mild weather, plenty of food and a nest site all in one area!

Maybe some of Stewart and Bell's babies will stay in Seattle, too.

Wouldn't that be nice?

Photo: C. M. Anderson

Photo: Patricia J. Hitchens

How can we help Seattle's skyscraper falcons?

We can help by not using poisons that hurt birds and other animals.

We can help by obeying laws that say not to shoot falcons.

We can help by learning about falcons and teaching others so that more people can enjoy them as much as we do.

Photos: Patricia J. Hitchens

Stewart and Bell have chosen Seattle for their home.

We hope that they will nest here for many years to come, so that they and their young will provide us with a skyscraper view of the remarkable life of peregrine falcons.

Glossary

banding—{BAND eeng} attaching a small, metal ring around a bird's leg. The band is numbered so that the bird can be identified.

barring—{BAR eeng} lines of color on a bird that are sideways. This is the opposite of streaking which goes up and down.

bird of prey—{burd uv pray} a bird with large eyes, sharp talons and a down-curved beak, that hunts and eats mainly meat. These include hawks, falcons, kites, harriers, eagles and owls.

brood—{brewd} sitting on the young to keep them warm.

captivity—{cap TIV it ee} in wild animals, not living free but in the care of people.

crop—{crop} a pouch in the neck of birds that is used for storing food.

down—{down} a covering of soft, fluffy feathers close to a bird's skin.

endangered species—{en DAYN jurd SPEE sheez} an animal group that is close to **extinction**.

extinction—{ek STINK shun} the death of an entire group of animals.

eyrie—{EYE ree} the nest of a bird of prey, usually a falcon or eagle.

eyass—{EYE us} a baby bird of prey before its first flight.

falcon—{FALL cun} a type of bird of prey. The female peregrine is also called a falcon (see **tiercel**).

fledgling—{FLEJ ling} a young bird after its first flight.

incubate—{INK u bate} to sit on eggs and keep them warm.

juvenile—{JOO ven ile} a fledged bird not yet in adult **plumage**.

malar—{MAL er} the dark streak on the cheek of falcons.

migrate—{MY grate} in falcons and many other birds, to travel south in fall and north in spring.

peregrine falcon—{PAIR a grin FALL cun} a swift bird of prey which mainly feeds on other birds.

plumage—{PLOO mij} all the feathers on a bird.

population—{pop u LAY shun} the total number of one kind of animal.

prey—{pray} an animal hunted by another animal for food.

scrape—{scrayp} a shallow hole on a falcon's nest ledgewhere the eggs are laid.

stoop—{stoop} in falcons, a swift downward dive (with wings folded in) to attack **prey**.

talon—{TAL uns} the claw of a falcon.

tiercel—{TEER sul} a male **peregrine falcon**.

VID band—{vee eye DEE band} a black band with two white letters for identifying individual birds.